Name

Email

This form is used to collect your name and email address so that I can add you to my mailing list and send you periodic newsletters. My newsletters usually focus on my books and my writing life.

☐ I consent to having my name and email address collected and retained for the purpose of communication

---

Name

Email

This form is used to collect your name and email address so that I can add you to my mailing list and send you periodic newsletters. My newsletters usually focus on my books and my writing life.

☐ I consent to having my name and email address collected and retained for the purpose of communication

Name

Email

This form is used to collect your name and email address so that I can add you to my mailing list and send you periodic newsletters. My newsletters usually focus on my books and my writing life.

☐ I consent to having my name and email address collected and retained for the purpose of communication

---

Name

Email

This form is used to collect your name and email address so that I can add you to my mailing list and send you periodic newsletters. My newsletters usually focus on my books and my writing life.

☐ I consent to having my name and email address collected and retained for the purpose of communication

Name

Email

This form is used to collect your name and email address so that I can add you to my mailing list and send you periodic newsletters. My newsletters usually focus on my books and my writing life.

☐ I consent to having my name and email address collected and retained for the purpose of communication

---

Name

Email

This form is used to collect your name and email address so that I can add you to my mailing list and send you periodic newsletters. My newsletters usually focus on my books and my writing life.

☐ I consent to having my name and email address collected and retained for the purpose of communication

Name

Email

This form is used to collect your name and email address so that I can add you to my mailing list and send you periodic newsletters. My newsletters usually focus on my books and my writing life.

☐ I consent to having my name and email address collected and retained for the purpose of communication

---

Name

Email

This form is used to collect your name and email address so that I can add you to my mailing list and send you periodic newsletters. My newsletters usually focus on my books and my writing life.

☐ I consent to having my name and email address collected and retained for the purpose of communication

Name

Email

This form is used to collect your name and email address so that I can add you to my mailing list and send you periodic newsletters. My newsletters usually focus on my books and my writing life.

☐ I consent to having my name and email address collected and retained for the purpose of communication

---

Name

Email

This form is used to collect your name and email address so that I can add you to my mailing list and send you periodic newsletters. My newsletters usually focus on my books and my writing life.

☐ I consent to having my name and email address collected and retained for the purpose of communication

Name

Email

This form is used to collect your name and email address so that I can add you to my mailing list and send you periodic newsletters. My newsletters usually focus on my books and my writing life.

☐ I consent to having my name and email address collected and retained for the purpose of communication

---

Name

Email

This form is used to collect your name and email address so that I can add you to my mailing list and send you periodic newsletters. My newsletters usually focus on my books and my writing life.

☐ I consent to having my name and email address collected and retained for the purpose of communication

Name

Email

This form is used to collect your name and email address so that I can add you to my mailing list and send you periodic newsletters. My newsletters usually focus on my books and my writing life.

☐ I consent to having my name and email address collected and retained for the purpose of communication

---

Name

Email

This form is used to collect your name and email address so that I can add you to my mailing list and send you periodic newsletters. My newsletters usually focus on my books and my writing life.

☐ I consent to having my name and email address collected and retained for the purpose of communication

Name

Email

This form is used to collect your name and email address so that I can add you to my mailing list and send you periodic newsletters. My newsletters usually focus on my books and my writing life.

☐ I consent to having my name and email address collected and retained for the purpose of communication

---

Name

Email

This form is used to collect your name and email address so that I can add you to my mailing list and send you periodic newsletters. My newsletters usually focus on my books and my writing life.

☐ I consent to having my name and email address collected and retained for the purpose of communication

Name

Email

This form is used to collect your name and email address so that I can add you to my mailing list and send you periodic newsletters. My newsletters usually focus on my books and my writing life.

☐ I consent to having my name and email address collected and retained for the purpose of communication

---

Name

Email

This form is used to collect your name and email address so that I can add you to my mailing list and send you periodic newsletters. My newsletters usually focus on my books and my writing life.

☐ I consent to having my name and email address collected and retained for the purpose of communication

Name

Email

This form is used to collect your name and email address so that I can add you to my mailing list and send you periodic newsletters. My newsletters usually focus on my books and my writing life.

☐ I consent to having my name and email address collected and retained for the purpose of communication

---

Name

Email

This form is used to collect your name and email address so that I can add you to my mailing list and send you periodic newsletters. My newsletters usually focus on my books and my writing life.

☐ I consent to having my name and email address collected and retained for the purpose of communication

Name

Email

This form is used to collect your name and email address so that I can add you to my mailing list and send you periodic newsletters. My newsletters usually focus on my books and my writing life.

☐ I consent to having my name and email address collected and retained for the purpose of communication

---

Name

Email

This form is used to collect your name and email address so that I can add you to my mailing list and send you periodic newsletters. My newsletters usually focus on my books and my writing life.

☐ I consent to having my name and email address collected and retained for the purpose of communication

Name

Email

This form is used to collect your name and email address so that I can add you to my mailing list and send you periodic newsletters. My newsletters usually focus on my books and my writing life.

☐ I consent to having my name and email address collected and retained for the purpose of communication

---

Name

Email

This form is used to collect your name and email address so that I can add you to my mailing list and send you periodic newsletters. My newsletters usually focus on my books and my writing life.

☐ I consent to having my name and email address collected and retained for the purpose of communication

Name

Email

This form is used to collect your name and email address so that I can add you to my mailing list and send you periodic newsletters. My newsletters usually focus on my books and my writing life.

☐ I consent to having my name and email address collected and retained for the purpose of communication

---

Name

Email

This form is used to collect your name and email address so that I can add you to my mailing list and send you periodic newsletters. My newsletters usually focus on my books and my writing life.

☐ I consent to having my name and email address collected and retained for the purpose of communication

Name

Email

This form is used to collect your name and email address so that I can add you to my mailing list and send you periodic newsletters. My newsletters usually focus on my books and my writing life.

☐ I consent to having my name and email address collected and retained for the purpose of communication

---

Name

Email

This form is used to collect your name and email address so that I can add you to my mailing list and send you periodic newsletters. My newsletters usually focus on my books and my writing life.

☐ I consent to having my name and email address collected and retained for the purpose of communication

Name

Email

This form is used to collect your name and email address so that I can add you to my mailing list and send you periodic newsletters. My newsletters usually focus on my books and my writing life.

☐ I consent to having my name and email address collected and retained for the purpose of communication

---

Name

Email

This form is used to collect your name and email address so that I can add you to my mailing list and send you periodic newsletters. My newsletters usually focus on my books and my writing life.

☐ I consent to having my name and email address collected and retained for the purpose of communication

Name

Email

This form is used to collect your name and email address so that I can add you to my mailing list and send you periodic newsletters. My newsletters usually focus on my books and my writing life.

☐ I consent to having my name and email address collected and retained for the purpose of communication

---

Name

Email

This form is used to collect your name and email address so that I can add you to my mailing list and send you periodic newsletters. My newsletters usually focus on my books and my writing life.

☐ I consent to having my name and email address collected and retained for the purpose of communication

Name

Email

This form is used to collect your name and email address so that I can add you to my mailing list and send you periodic newsletters. My newsletters usually focus on my books and my writing life.

☐ I consent to having my name and email address collected and retained for the purpose of communication

---

Name

Email

This form is used to collect your name and email address so that I can add you to my mailing list and send you periodic newsletters. My newsletters usually focus on my books and my writing life.

☐ I consent to having my name and email address collected and retained for the purpose of communication

Name

Email

This form is used to collect your name and email address so that I can add you to my mailing list and send you periodic newsletters. My newsletters usually focus on my books and my writing life.

☐ I consent to having my name and email address collected and retained for the purpose of communication

---

Name

Email

This form is used to collect your name and email address so that I can add you to my mailing list and send you periodic newsletters. My newsletters usually focus on my books and my writing life.

☐ I consent to having my name and email address collected and retained for the purpose of communication

Name

Email

This form is used to collect your name and email address so that I can add you to my mailing list and send you periodic newsletters. My newsletters usually focus on my books and my writing life.

☐ I consent to having my name and email address collected and retained for the purpose of communication

---

Name

Email

This form is used to collect your name and email address so that I can add you to my mailing list and send you periodic newsletters. My newsletters usually focus on my books and my writing life.

☐ I consent to having my name and email address collected and retained for the purpose of communication

Name

Email

This form is used to collect your name and email address so that I can add you to my mailing list and send you periodic newsletters. My newsletters usually focus on my books and my writing life.

☐ I consent to having my name and email address collected and retained for the purpose of communication

---

Name

Email

This form is used to collect your name and email address so that I can add you to my mailing list and send you periodic newsletters. My newsletters usually focus on my books and my writing life.

☐ I consent to having my name and email address collected and retained for the purpose of communication

Name

Email

This form is used to collect your name and email address so that I can add you to my mailing list and send you periodic newsletters. My newsletters usually focus on my books and my writing life.

☐ I consent to having my name and email address collected and retained for the purpose of communication

---

Name

Email

This form is used to collect your name and email address so that I can add you to my mailing list and send you periodic newsletters. My newsletters usually focus on my books and my writing life.

☐ I consent to having my name and email address collected and retained for the purpose of communication

Name

Email

This form is used to collect your name and email address so that I can add you to my mailing list and send you periodic newsletters. My newsletters usually focus on my books and my writing life.

☐ I consent to having my name and email address collected and retained for the purpose of communication

---

Name

Email

This form is used to collect your name and email address so that I can add you to my mailing list and send you periodic newsletters. My newsletters usually focus on my books and my writing life.

☐ I consent to having my name and email address collected and retained for the purpose of communication

Name

Email

This form is used to collect your name and email address so that I can add you to my mailing list and send you periodic newsletters. My newsletters usually focus on my books and my writing life.

☐ I consent to having my name and email address collected and retained for the purpose of communication

---

Name

Email

This form is used to collect your name and email address so that I can add you to my mailing list and send you periodic newsletters. My newsletters usually focus on my books and my writing life.

☐ I consent to having my name and email address collected and retained for the purpose of communication

Name

Email

This form is used to collect your name and email address so that I can add you to my mailing list and send you periodic newsletters. My newsletters usually focus on my books and my writing life.

☐ I consent to having my name and email address collected and retained for the purpose of communication

---

Name

Email

This form is used to collect your name and email address so that I can add you to my mailing list and send you periodic newsletters. My newsletters usually focus on my books and my writing life.

☐ I consent to having my name and email address collected and retained for the purpose of communication

Name

Email

This form is used to collect your name and email address so that I can add you to my mailing list and send you periodic newsletters. My newsletters usually focus on my books and my writing life.

☐ I consent to having my name and email address collected and retained for the purpose of communication

---

Name

Email

This form is used to collect your name and email address so that I can add you to my mailing list and send you periodic newsletters. My newsletters usually focus on my books and my writing life.

☐ I consent to having my name and email address collected and retained for the purpose of communication

Name

Email

This form is used to collect your name and email address so that I can add you to my mailing list and send you periodic newsletters. My newsletters usually focus on my books and my writing life.

☐ I consent to having my name and email address collected and retained for the purpose of communication

---

Name

Email

This form is used to collect your name and email address so that I can add you to my mailing list and send you periodic newsletters. My newsletters usually focus on my books and my writing life.

☐ I consent to having my name and email address collected and retained for the purpose of communication

Name

Email

This form is used to collect your name and email address so that I can add you to my mailing list and send you periodic newsletters. My newsletters usually focus on my books and my writing life.

☐ I consent to having my name and email address collected and retained for the purpose of communication

---

Name

Email

This form is used to collect your name and email address so that I can add you to my mailing list and send you periodic newsletters. My newsletters usually focus on my books and my writing life.

☐ I consent to having my name and email address collected and retained for the purpose of communication

Name

Email

This form is used to collect your name and email address so that I can add you to my mailing list and send you periodic newsletters. My newsletters usually focus on my books and my writing life.

☐ I consent to having my name and email address collected and retained for the purpose of communication

---

Name

Email

This form is used to collect your name and email address so that I can add you to my mailing list and send you periodic newsletters. My newsletters usually focus on my books and my writing life.

☐ I consent to having my name and email address collected and retained for the purpose of communication

Name

Email

This form is used to collect your name and email address so that I can add you to my mailing list and send you periodic newsletters. My newsletters usually focus on my books and my writing life.

☐ I consent to having my name and email address collected and retained for the purpose of communication

---

Name

Email

This form is used to collect your name and email address so that I can add you to my mailing list and send you periodic newsletters. My newsletters usually focus on my books and my writing life.

☐ I consent to having my name and email address collected and retained for the purpose of communication

Name

Email

This form is used to collect your name and email address so that I can add you to my mailing list and send you periodic newsletters. My newsletters usually focus on my books and my writing life.

☐ I consent to having my name and email address collected and retained for the purpose of communication

---

Name

Email

This form is used to collect your name and email address so that I can add you to my mailing list and send you periodic newsletters. My newsletters usually focus on my books and my writing life.

☐ I consent to having my name and email address collected and retained for the purpose of communication

Name

Email

This form is used to collect your name and email address so that I can add you to my mailing list and send you periodic newsletters. My newsletters usually focus on my books and my writing life.

☐ I consent to having my name and email address collected and retained for the purpose of communication

---

Name

Email

This form is used to collect your name and email address so that I can add you to my mailing list and send you periodic newsletters. My newsletters usually focus on my books and my writing life.

☐ I consent to having my name and email address collected and retained for the purpose of communication

Name

Email

This form is used to collect your name and email address so that I can add you to my mailing list and send you periodic newsletters. My newsletters usually focus on my books and my writing life.

☐ I consent to having my name and email address collected and retained for the purpose of communication

---

Name

Email

This form is used to collect your name and email address so that I can add you to my mailing list and send you periodic newsletters. My newsletters usually focus on my books and my writing life.

☐ I consent to having my name and email address collected and retained for the purpose of communication

Name

Email

This form is used to collect your name and email address so that I can add you to my mailing list and send you periodic newsletters. My newsletters usually focus on my books and my writing life.

☐ I consent to having my name and email address collected and retained for the purpose of communication

---

Name

Email

This form is used to collect your name and email address so that I can add you to my mailing list and send you periodic newsletters. My newsletters usually focus on my books and my writing life.

☐ I consent to having my name and email address collected and retained for the purpose of communication

Name

Email

This form is used to collect your name and email address so that I can add you to my mailing list and send you periodic newsletters. My newsletters usually focus on my books and my writing life.

☐ I consent to having my name and email address collected and retained for the purpose of communication

---

Name

Email

This form is used to collect your name and email address so that I can add you to my mailing list and send you periodic newsletters. My newsletters usually focus on my books and my writing life.

☐ I consent to having my name and email address collected and retained for the purpose of communication

Name

Email

This form is used to collect your name and email address so that I can add you to my mailing list and send you periodic newsletters. My newsletters usually focus on my books and my writing life.

☐ I consent to having my name and email address collected and retained for the purpose of communication

---

Name

Email

This form is used to collect your name and email address so that I can add you to my mailing list and send you periodic newsletters. My newsletters usually focus on my books and my writing life.

☐ I consent to having my name and email address collected and retained for the purpose of communication

Name

Email

This form is used to collect your name and email address so that I can add you to my mailing list and send you periodic newsletters. My newsletters usually focus on my books and my writing life.

☐ I consent to having my name and email address collected and retained for the purpose of communication

---

Name

Email

This form is used to collect your name and email address so that I can add you to my mailing list and send you periodic newsletters. My newsletters usually focus on my books and my writing life.

☐ I consent to having my name and email address collected and retained for the purpose of communication

Name

Email

This form is used to collect your name and email address so that I can add you to my mailing list and send you periodic newsletters. My newsletters usually focus on my books and my writing life.

☐ I consent to having my name and email address collected and retained for the purpose of communication

---

Name

Email

This form is used to collect your name and email address so that I can add you to my mailing list and send you periodic newsletters. My newsletters usually focus on my books and my writing life.

☐ I consent to having my name and email address collected and retained for the purpose of communication

Name

Email

This form is used to collect your name and email address so that I can add you to my mailing list and send you periodic newsletters. My newsletters usually focus on my books and my writing life.

☐ I consent to having my name and email address collected and retained for the purpose of communication

---

Name

Email

This form is used to collect your name and email address so that I can add you to my mailing list and send you periodic newsletters. My newsletters usually focus on my books and my writing life.

☐ I consent to having my name and email address collected and retained for the purpose of communication

Name

Email

This form is used to collect your name and email address so that I can add you to my mailing list and send you periodic newsletters. My newsletters usually focus on my books and my writing life.

☐ I consent to having my name and email address collected and retained for the purpose of communication

Name

Email

This form is used to collect your name and email address so that I can add you to my mailing list and send you periodic newsletters. My newsletters usually focus on my books and my writing life.

☐ I consent to having my name and email address collected and retained for the purpose of communication

Name

Email

This form is used to collect your name and email address so that I can add you to my mailing list and send you periodic newsletters. My newsletters usually focus on my books and my writing life.

☐ I consent to having my name and email address collected and retained for the purpose of communication

---

Name

Email

This form is used to collect your name and email address so that I can add you to my mailing list and send you periodic newsletters. My newsletters usually focus on my books and my writing life.

☐ I consent to having my name and email address collected and retained for the purpose of communication

Name

Email

This form is used to collect your name and email address so that I can add you to my mailing list and send you periodic newsletters. My newsletters usually focus on my books and my writing life.

☐ I consent to having my name and email address collected and retained for the purpose of communication

---

Name

Email

This form is used to collect your name and email address so that I can add you to my mailing list and send you periodic newsletters. My newsletters usually focus on my books and my writing life.

☐ I consent to having my name and email address collected and retained for the purpose of communication

Name

Email

This form is used to collect your name and email address so that I can add you to my mailing list and send you periodic newsletters. My newsletters usually focus on my books and my writing life.

☐ I consent to having my name and email address collected and retained for the purpose of communication

---

Name

Email

This form is used to collect your name and email address so that I can add you to my mailing list and send you periodic newsletters. My newsletters usually focus on my books and my writing life.

☐ I consent to having my name and email address collected and retained for the purpose of communication

Name

Email

This form is used to collect your name and email address so that I can add you to my mailing list and send you periodic newsletters. My newsletters usually focus on my books and my writing life.

☐ I consent to having my name and email address collected and retained for the purpose of communication

---

Name

Email

This form is used to collect your name and email address so that I can add you to my mailing list and send you periodic newsletters. My newsletters usually focus on my books and my writing life.

☐ I consent to having my name and email address collected and retained for the purpose of communication

Name

Email

This form is used to collect your name and email address so that I can add you to my mailing list and send you periodic newsletters. My newsletters usually focus on my books and my writing life.

☐ I consent to having my name and email address collected and retained for the purpose of communication

---

Name

Email

This form is used to collect your name and email address so that I can add you to my mailing list and send you periodic newsletters. My newsletters usually focus on my books and my writing life.

☐ I consent to having my name and email address collected and retained for the purpose of communication

Name

Email

This form is used to collect your name and email address so that I can add you to my mailing list and send you periodic newsletters. My newsletters usually focus on my books and my writing life.

☐ I consent to having my name and email address collected and retained for the purpose of communication

---

Name

Email

This form is used to collect your name and email address so that I can add you to my mailing list and send you periodic newsletters. My newsletters usually focus on my books and my writing life.

☐ I consent to having my name and email address collected and retained for the purpose of communication

Name

Email

This form is used to collect your name and email address so that I can add you to my mailing list and send you periodic newsletters. My newsletters usually focus on my books and my writing life.

☐ I consent to having my name and email address collected and retained for the purpose of communication

---

Name

Email

This form is used to collect your name and email address so that I can add you to my mailing list and send you periodic newsletters. My newsletters usually focus on my books and my writing life.

☐ I consent to having my name and email address collected and retained for the purpose of communication

Name

Email

This form is used to collect your name and email address so that I can add you to my mailing list and send you periodic newsletters. My newsletters usually focus on my books and my writing life.

☐ I consent to having my name and email address collected and retained for the purpose of communication

---

Name

Email

This form is used to collect your name and email address so that I can add you to my mailing list and send you periodic newsletters. My newsletters usually focus on my books and my writing life.

☐ I consent to having my name and email address collected and retained for the purpose of communication

Name

Email

This form is used to collect your name and email address so that I can add you to my mailing list and send you periodic newsletters. My newsletters usually focus on my books and my writing life.

☐ I consent to having my name and email address collected and retained for the purpose of communication

---

Name

Email

This form is used to collect your name and email address so that I can add you to my mailing list and send you periodic newsletters. My newsletters usually focus on my books and my writing life.

☐ I consent to having my name and email address collected and retained for the purpose of communication

Name

Email

This form is used to collect your name and email address so that I can add you to my mailing list and send you periodic newsletters. My newsletters usually focus on my books and my writing life.

☐ I consent to having my name and email address collected and retained for the purpose of communication

---

Name

Email

This form is used to collect your name and email address so that I can add you to my mailing list and send you periodic newsletters. My newsletters usually focus on my books and my writing life.

☐ I consent to having my name and email address collected and retained for the purpose of communication

Name

Email

This form is used to collect your name and email address so that I can add you to my mailing list and send you periodic newsletters. My newsletters usually focus on my books and my writing life.

☐ I consent to having my name and email address collected and retained for the purpose of communication

---

Name

Email

This form is used to collect your name and email address so that I can add you to my mailing list and send you periodic newsletters. My newsletters usually focus on my books and my writing life.

☐ I consent to having my name and email address collected and retained for the purpose of communication

Name

Email

This form is used to collect your name and email address so that I can add you to my mailing list and send you periodic newsletters. My newsletters usually focus on my books and my writing life.

☐ I consent to having my name and email address collected and retained for the purpose of communication

---

Name

Email

This form is used to collect your name and email address so that I can add you to my mailing list and send you periodic newsletters. My newsletters usually focus on my books and my writing life.

☐ I consent to having my name and email address collected and retained for the purpose of communication

www.ingramcontent.com/pod-product-compliance
Lightning Source LLC
Chambersburg PA
CBHW081202020426
42333CB00020B/2591